To John . . .

"Come walk with me
as One
beyond the shadow
called tomorrow
through Our Inner Voice."

Your friend

Robert James Bearns

I've longed you like a blind man
hungers darkness into ...
light ...

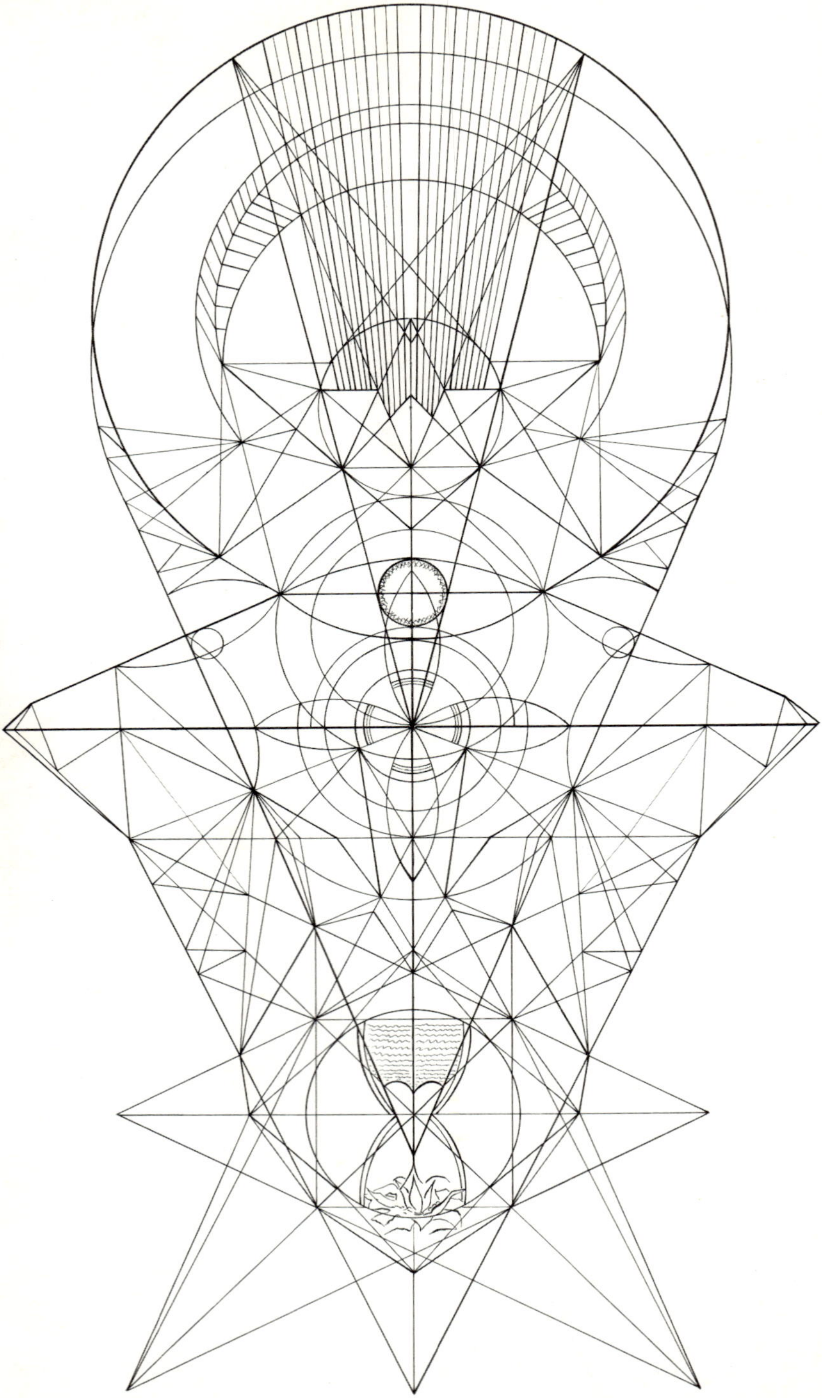

Out of darkness
came a voice
voiced by two friends
... unknown ...

Distance played itself
voicing
voicing the friend
he would come to know

Out of darkness
came his voice
HIS INNER VOICE
to say hello

If I be here or gone ...
you were always the one
I believed one day would come

If I screamed too loud
or frightened you from within ...
it was only my loneliness trying
to awaken you

You I've loved
You I've lived

It's been whispered aloud by those who
say they know you, " 'Twould be better
off you be ridden as an ass."

Who are you that I should need you so?

It is not the wishbone of your hips my
harpoon desires saddled, but the bridaling
of your mind in the here and now. A
spiritual alignment, a touching crossing
the threshold, fathoming together its true
depths, a sirened call mooring a landing.

They, whoever they are, dismiss you as
hunger driven, bedded only by the flesh,
cankered.

I choose to believe them wrong.

Children see, and ask, but question not
where love is housed, nor do those who
read between the lines. And their silence
far outweighs your dismissal.

My penn would have little to offer were
vanity or the loss of humility venturing
a footprint, coining a story one-sided.
Nor would it desire you — unfree — without
the self questioning its two sides.
You have one face; *i* am faceless.

Were you to look
You'd find me afoot
Autumned in the leaf
Upon the raft
Everest its climb

Were you to look
Now that you're here
Will you care why I cared
Loved ... and thought ...
About your arrival

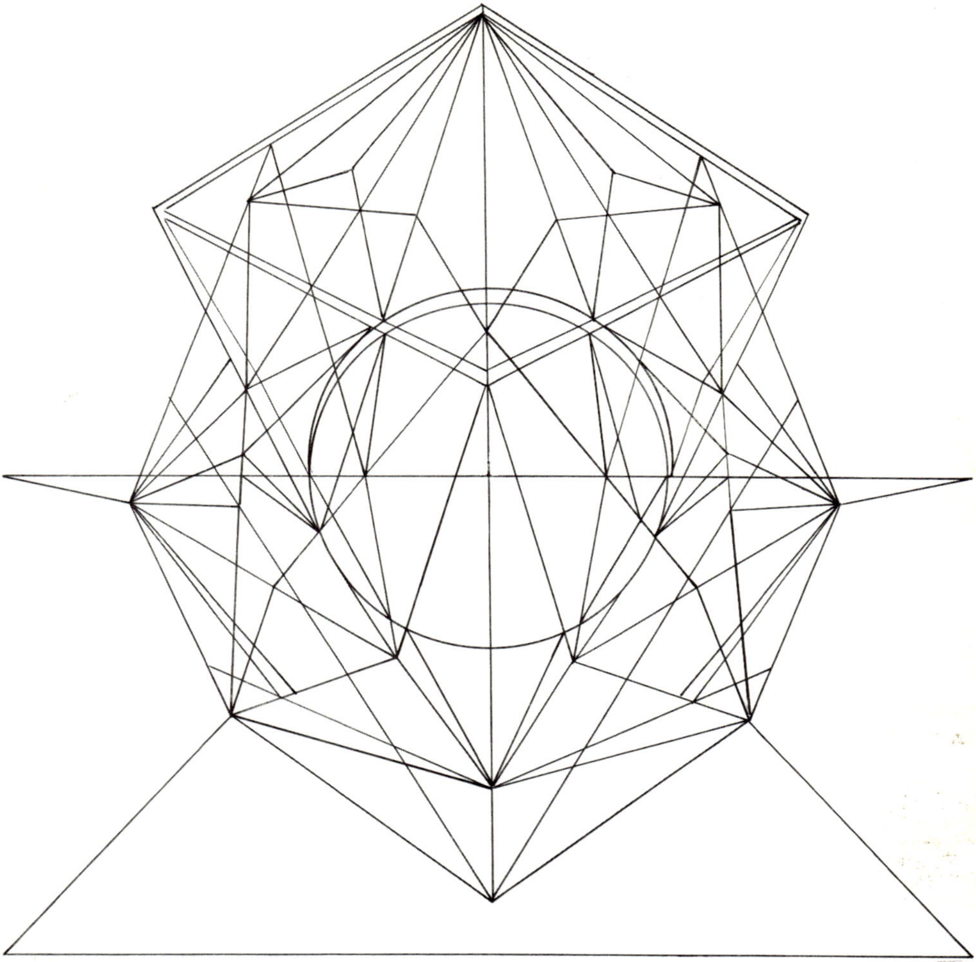

DEDICATED to One
One who needs me
Within this One
One love I am

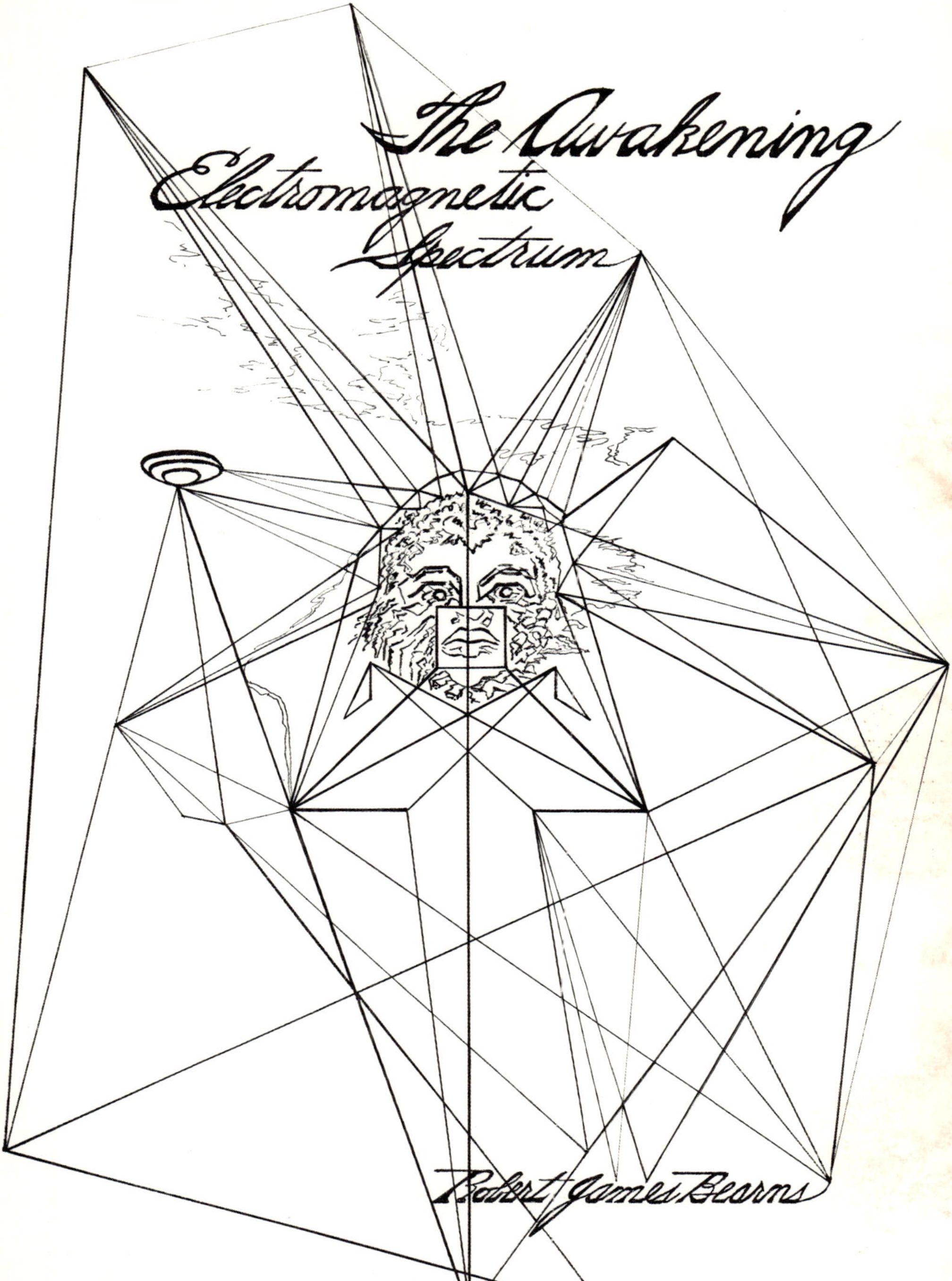
The Awakening
Electromagnetic
Spectrum
Robert James Bearns

All drawings and lyrics
appearing in this book
were also signatured by
the author's penn.

AWAKENING PRODUCTIONS
1632 Vallejo, #5
San Francisco, California 94123

ISBN 0-914 7 06-00- 4
Library of Congress card number: 74-76050
Manufactured in the United States of America
Printed by Phelps/Schaefer Litho-graphics Co.

THE HEXAGRAM

Scrolls before you humanitarian nakedness
To others it might appear as ridiculous
as balancing an egg on a turtle's back

What comprises a writer

How does the shadow of his penn
move across the barren white pages
leaving his thought tracks

The road he travels
is but his own awakening
He himself must be the first
to taste of its nectar
It in itself
the blind road

The original words of authors past
he needs as fertilization into his ground
seeking through the hardest of stone
the truth ... the halo vein ... The Mother Lode
if truth be the author's penn

I cannot say unto you
if my penn speaks only the truth
as you are always the Mother Lode it but seeks

I shall spend my life longing you.
Within the silence of my heart
will drum aloud the sweet sound
of your applause
if truth be fulfilled
in the dipping of my penn

To lay an egg
not easy
Harder still
to crack it from within

The Hexagram
of the Electromagnetic Spectrum

He who carries
no key
Seeks no door be closed
There his coming and going are One

THE MOMENT

I but took the moment and danced with it
    as it moved itself 'round me like a flame
And there I danced in silence

My penn now dipping of itself
    like a monkey playing throughout a tree
Balancing thought from hand to hand

As I but suckled the naked nipple of life
    tasting of its truth ...
How pleased the feeling

I tasted my thoughts, bowed my arrow
    ... and stepped aside

The judging of my *penn* will come not by one who quickly passes, listens, and moves on.

As a pyramid has a beginning, the onlooking eye cannot weather its seasonal change, but should enjoy the very thought of its conception.

If the idea be made of clay, its pigment will not withstand, but fade into the sands of time, and there shall be no judging.

Time, as known, will pass into a new Awakening; its judging will withstand a lifetime of goodbyes, welcoming new hellos.

Let the pages be turned anew, levitating a truthful page for the next to turn .... As You, She, He, *i*, It, or Zero shall one day return, pilot the astral center ♒ lotusing the page you turn.

Robert James Bearns

We're going on a voyage, a journey through air and space beyond this moment in time.

There will be little needed beyond belief ≈≈ proprietorship to the moment of departure, rendering fear a moment's rest, between conventional rules of behavior.

A voyage ... set apart for a specific purpose, destination unlimited ... destination known.

Let your eye of awareness through your

INNER VOICE

BE YOUR GUIDE

IN THE LIFTING OF THE MASK ....

TOMORROW'S STRAIGHT AHEAD
WHY LINGER YESTERDAY ...

ZERO

While looking at one's self reclining
From across the room
You but fade into the total energy
No more, no less, than a spectrum
Of the total awareness

Like a kaleidoscope wheel
Moving in two different directions
Between the third and fourth dimension

In order to project, you see them as *One*
The mind stops time — and you move through
Losing one's self unto one's self
Finding one within *One*
Total …
ZERO

THE SILENT BREATH

I shall be as mute as the silent breath
which never takes of itself ...
CONCEPTION

I shall be as mute as darkness —
that which seeks its own light ...
BIRTH

I shall run the circle wind a race
and win, and win.
The silent breath I shall begin ...
LIFE

THE EYE OF THE HURRICANE

That year, it seemed we must have flown a thousand kites. Every dream we set aloft in search of a higher balance. How many, many times they fell to the ground, and together we picked them up and off we sailed them again. Even through hidden tears we recognized the growth needed in the time zone, and would toast a laugh, seeing the brighter side of the day. The eye of the hurricane became our sanctuary and from within its stillness we'd weather out the storms. Beyond ourselves ... our banner we held aloft to win.

Life was no longer played out as a passing game, but the play itself. We allied the moon, lensing its changes, and developed the negative into the positive upon its face. The stiffness in our voices gave way to confidence, rendering belief before our eyes. Like children, we reached out to touch the golden ring.

To have played the game in the name of self only, would have dried the well, muting it of its true soundings. Faceless faces took on new meaning while other hands readied themselves. A once dreamed platform became a living reality. Surfacing our lost yesterdays we unlodged the fermented wisdom of our years, freeing anew upon this platform our songs ... winging them homeward.

Little beyond belief flowers in the garden, and the void stretches a pathway for the seeding. Tomorrow after tomorrow, together we shall walk, and like children upon the hillside, we shall run our kites.

Once there was a time
A thought — a word — a rhyme
Were eager to be bedded

Oh to live the time
When man gave himself to rhyme
A rhyme — a word — a thought
Was all he needed

The quietest of word
Could shed a laugh, a tear
Roar an eardrum from its sleep
Once there was a time
A thought — a word — a rhyme
Was all he needed

But now a sneeze
Is closer to the head
Listening to the fallout ashes
Of an empty heart
Losing step with its drummer
Never hearing the faint sound
Of a child bathing his face
In a smile

Who'll take the time
Who'll take the time
To walk with me through a rhyme
I've love to give if you've the time
If you've the time
... Once there was a time

Faceless
    may appear the day
    in its passing
The ladder
    too many steps
    to climb
The sea
    will never run away
    from its shore

Beyond the self
    lies greatness
Success hovers
    the envisioned
Learning
    true distance
From whence
    the Seed abides

Many mansions palimpsest

Thunder thy lost cities
    Beneath thy sea ... *rise*

Come forth live again

Is not a chain a link
    Unto itself ...

From where one fathoms
    The moorings

Drags the chain link ... by ... link

THE WATCH

Time, you but hold the watch —
        I'll not return

... But I've a *RHYME* if you've the time

A walnut on a tree I see
        Come ... look
Greener the pod than yesterday's shadow
Warmer the fall than the winds of tomorrow

I've a rhyme if you've the time
I've a rhyme if you've the time

A walnut now on the ground you see
Drying in the dust of time to set it free
Come look, if you've the time —
        Come
I'll keep the watch

STILL AND ALL

Waves upon the shore
Rainbow chasing
Mosquito clapping ...
        waves upon the shore

Silent the study
Lights glaring paper
        MOSQUITO
        ... studied ...
                coffee
                thought
                time
        ... cat box scratching
Nothing said

Still and all
        mosquito clapping ...
Waves upon the shore

TWELVE STEPS

in the ladder

all twelve needing

to be climbed ...   One Step ... In Step ... One Step at a time

Why rush the boy within the man

He has a right to live there a lifetime ...

As a child, I ran the beanfields, caring little about growing up. I had a horse named Rusty and he was all the world to me. I loved him so much, I never accepted the truth — he was old and half blind. All I knew ... I loved him so much.

Time spins a boy into manhood by reflecting new dreams, and one day I turned the key, starting up my first jalopy, and raced headlong into girls and love affairs.

Little of life has found me empty even though often I've been called a dreamer. I still love my yesterdays and light the candle of remembrance within the warehouse.

Now that autumn has faded, winter's whiteness has reached my brow, reflecting the distance — the true distance upon my walk. To run the beanfields, to ride the merry-go-round, to reach out and touch the ring of life has always been my dream. Little boys grow up, pretty girls turn them into men, but only the love of life ... *only* the love of life, forever renews the boy within the man.

SELF PITY

The transformation through the positive force-field relinquishes its hold on the negative called *self pity*.

How well we who have adorned our faces with his ugly mask know his hiding place. *For those who walk beyond his calling, linger not a moment.*

I'll write all I can find within myself to be true, one day removing my penn to rest in its words. *And just what is truth?* Moreover, what am I?

Sometimes, it's easy to write all the beautiful thoughts that roll a dream into color. But *truth*, as known, sits not alone on the colorful throne of life.

Let's take a good look at his other face:

Tense
Drawn
Eyes hollow
Energy building up
... and nowhere to go!

Don't kid yourself, if you've never been a visitor in the house of *self pity* — stay out! He who sees beyond the self sees another's need, renouncing *self pity. The unknown deeper sleeps.*

Many a beautiful mind knows the passing of unfulfilled dreams, lingers not the thought, but dreams anew. Cries heard in *self pity,* voicing unto itself, ever-tighten the decaying mask.

He who sees beyond himself sees:

Happiness

A THOUGHT

Have you dropped
Or misplaced
A thought along the way

From where you stand
Could it be retrieved
Or has distance lost its need

Or has the broom
Standing center
Clearing the walls
Transcended a dust pan

A hen-pecked man
Is like a dried out fruitcake
Cackled by a heavy-footed hen

The more she pecks
The better he likes it
Till she pockets his money
And flies the pen

Watched a man blowin' steam
locked up in a traffic jam
horns honkin'
nerves crackin'
drivin' nails
boardin' up a no-way man

Watched a woman flyin' her gums
locked up in a traffic jam
horns honkin'
nerves crackin'
drivin' nails
boardin' up a no-way woman
boardin' up a no-way man

Saw a bird takin' wing
Watched a tortoise win a race
horns honkin'
nerves crackin'
drivin' nails
boardin' up the human race

Watched a child fly his kite
... what more can I say ...

SILENCE

Silence is the sound
Known to the lonely
A world within a world
All its own

Silence is the sound of tears
Or a child not loved
Lost in the playground
The playground of the mind

There are those who hide in the crowd
And laugh out loud, never hearing
The lonely heartbreak of another
Only to learn after many a careless laugh
Up pops the joker full circle
And then and there the fiddler must be paid

The loneliest of the lonely
The elderly
Those who are being passed by
Stare time ... dusting through memories

Yes, silence is the sound of tears
Or a child not loved

few sounds race the mind
caging innocence as do those
expressed by the bully
        eyes glaring venom
        ego riding fast its laughter
                its retreat

by its glare so shall it mirror the self

shadowing his knees
the sandy haired boy
holding a broken friend

prismed eyes
searching the *why*
spoke-kicked wheels
destroyed
his long awaited
new friend

the bully

Stand in the clearing ...

And in the *C-L-E-A-R-I-N-G*

You Shall See

You've changed
You truly have
Time has had its way with you

You're more handsomely beautiful
Than I'd remembered

NOT BY CHANCE

We meet not by chance
Nor need our meeting fade
We meet not by chance
But out of love for one another

Tomorrow would have been too late
Facelessly we've passed too often
In the light of our love
Now is all there need be

Had the days not run away so fast
Had the nights not found me alone
Or had I known the mystery
To stopping time was just by saying ...
hello

Had I known you desired me
Or even wished I'd speak my name
I'd have come forward ... touched you
Loved you ...
long before this

THE LAMP

For me you have set a table
        Your lamp has crackled a melody

From whence we speak
        Distance has lost its meaning

For me you have set a table
        Spoonerismed a broth
        A nourishing

Your lamp has crackled a melody
        Giving me a song to sing

THE GIANT SURF

The giant surf thrusted his wave deep
The undulating sand buoyanted her shores
Every pebble stone rock and boulder
She placed at her command

Onward the giant surf came
And again she coiled
Like a thundering stallion riding full herd
He mounted her

Again she coiled
Roping his seaweed full circle
She quicksanded him
Nectared her palate
Spawned her eggs
Readied herself
And again, onward he came

outside dampness falls
heavy rain
warmly my bed holds me
captive
too soon time will ring
outing the day bird
from his cage

MISTER HE CALLED ME

"Mister"
    he called me
with his bright little face
shining up from ever-so-far-down below

"Mister"
    he called me
while stumbling, tumbling
playing my path, hugging himself
'round my knees

"Mister, do you ever laugh? Do you, mister?
    Mister, do you? Do you ever laugh?"

    DO I EVER LAUGH? Why, do I ever laugh?
    Do I ... ever ... do I ... do I ever laugh?

"Mister, do you ever sing? Do you, mister?
    Mister, do you? Do you ever sing?"

    DO I EVER SING? Why, do I ever sing?
    Do I ... ever ... do I ... do I ever sing?

Quicker the shadow he ran on
Quicker he was gone

Drier my voice than when he found me
Alive again, tasted the tear
Now rolling my cheek

"Mister"
    he called me
with his *WONDERFUL* bright little face

The very edge of the day
May find a man
Weary, tired, and worn
From pulling a plow
Others feel should be drawn
Only by an ass

When the furrows he foots
Seed his daily dreams
He should be the judge
If the yoke but chokes
Its carrier

Too many dreams are lost
When sifted through another's hands

IT'S NOT NECESSARY TO QUESTION

A DEED WELL DONE

IT BALANCES ITSELF

IN ITS OWN WEIGHT

A three-sided story
A triangle
All three sides One
One and the same
A triangle

Tolerance Patience Understanding

1. Tolerance Understanding Patience

2. Patience Understanding Tolerance

3. Understanding Understanding Understanding

A three-sided story
A triangle ...
Understanding

THE NEWBORN

Unlike the newborn chick
        I but scratch my surface

The newborn knows the corn grows
        beneath his feet
                He asks not *why*
                        but scratches

Oh but to give myself to my ground
        dare I fear the worm
                the worm of darkness

The newborn hungers
        always hungers by the day

I but scratch my surface

EMOTION

Any set of good musicians
can play the composition
but that's not where it's at

The emotion is the ingredient
that cannot be written down

It's the unheard smile or laugh
sung by the one face
unto the other
at the very moment of excitement

Acceleration of love
in the brotherhood of achievement
that sings aloud ... never seen
only felt by the listener

That which gives us truth
of the spontaneity
of the moment
of creation

HUMAN BONDAGE

Lyrics ... lyrics ... lyrics
Proclaiming the Light
Crying out to be bedded

Music more so than ever before plays a dramatic role in our lives. World-wide we hear our contemporary composers awakening the Seed of Understanding. The truth hides not from he who seeks its awareness. A universal voice beckons, needing to be properly collaged and sifted. A forward road held open, not only to the young. The decoding of the lyric has freed many an enslaved soul lost in bondage, listening out the truth sitting a two-sided throne.

Lyrics ... lyrics ... lyrics ... crying out to be bedded — synthesizing, paletting color, brightening the darkest of days.

It's a summer storm
Not that it's gonna' rain
It's a summer storm
It's passing through the thunder
On its way out to sea
It's a summer storm
One day we knew might appear
No reason to run
It's passing through the thunder
Soon the clouds will disappear
SEE THE NEW LIGHT
SEE THE NEW LIGHT

Man, believing the self to be evolving his rightful humanitarian awareness, faces now the self adorned in a plastic facade called happiness. Nakedly, we face together an acceleration from within the mind's eye, crossing life's threshold through the Awakening Electromagnetic Spectrum.

A fourth dimensional lensing
envisioned by
a twenty-first century awareness

The very thought compels us to question our position. A world devastated by the blistered seam of aggression paralyzes the onlooking eye. Its overpowering generators needle the marrow from within our bones, ever-weakening our world's nervous system. A tonality heard through a warped harp played by the hand of a gorilla.

This lyrical ballad, decoded, walks its listener through a hell-like maze, disabling him from keeping step with his rightful drummer.

Hand in hand, we together have reached the end of a yesterday road, facing now a force field devastated by the atom: a pregnability conceivable only through the mind seeded in love.

We've passed the point of no return
And what seemed impossible
Is now beginning to appear
The road hasn't been easy
Often we've lost our way
But doubt never crossed our pathway
SEE THE NEW LIGHT
SEE THE NEW LIGHT
We've passed the point of no return
Together, together we're going home

Listen out the lyrics sung by nature. She adorns her garden, breasting the onlooking eye in a variety of colors, seen nakedly true through the eyes of a child.

FLOWERS OF OUR CHILDHOOD

It is not the child who is blind
but we who can no longer see
the flowers of our childhood

It is not the child who is mute
but we who can no longer hear
the song of life singing

    I ran so fast after my kite
    thinking I had lost it
    and then I stumbled
    … and in that moment
    I rooted my ground
                freeing myself …
    while watching the distance
    between our detachment
    play itself

It is not the child who is lost
but we who have turned from
the true pathway leading home

It is not the child who is blind
mute or lost
but we who can no longer hear
the song of life singing

MAMA, it's not your smile
I remember
MAMA, it's not your voice
It's just you, *MAMA*
It's just you

DADDY, it's not your laugh
I remember
DADDY, it's not your eyes
It's just you, *DADDY*
It's just you

Little boys grow up one day
And hide themselves away
Little girls dress up one day
And bloom April into May

Before your eyes now stands the man
Schooled, polished, and veneered
Before your eyes now stands the woman
Breasting life — renewing your yesteryears

Even though I've always told you
I thought you'd like to know
MAMA
DADDY
... I love you so

THE VIRGIN

The flowering within
Weakens the outer walls
Canyoned turbulence explored
Trembles the young unknown

Lullaby muted breasts
Cradled softly in a pillow
While awareness erupts
The turbulent canyon
In a dream

A love heard in silence
Bursting forth the woman
Flowering her full bloom
By early spring

Trembles the young woman
Canyon explored … held lost
To the arms of her lover
Forever lost the virgin …
Awakens the virgin spring

listened voices were singing
a *Hummingbird*
a *Cricket*
a *Butterfly*
and then there was you
and the little *Nat* • al … dotting the *i*

THE HUNTERS

Like all hunters
I too stalk my prey
Like all hunters of the flesh
I too wear a mask
Only wearier of it
By the day

Like all hunters
I too need to be bedded
You tonight ... who tomorrow?
And so the hunt goes on

Like all hunters of the flesh
I too must face the day
When the masquerade is over

One day ... one day
I must give way
My hunting ground
To younger
As one who lived, hunted
And wearied of the game

Unto the unknown's house came ... *AGING*. Knowing not what to do, he but meditated, losing thought unto thought as it hung heavy on his door. The unknown, having not prepared, problemed now the lodging of his new arrival, and found he had but barred himself against the door. Again his thoughts went 'round and 'round, while within a crack throughout the door *AGING* slowly crept — welcomed himself from within, ever watching the unknown bar the door.

THE MUSTARD SEED

I've longed you like a blind man hungers darkness
into light. I've asked the wind to search you, and
for every artery to lead you to the great stream.
Every storm I've cleared through the wings of gulls
... and never did I wonder your return.

In my mind's eye, in the dead of winter,
we walked and talked upon the summer's green,
and together we tended the mustard seed
... and never did I wonder your return.

Tomorrow will be soon enough to know the unknown
answers. In our closeness, in our love, let us
believe. I will not ask you to walk where I will
not lead. Nor will I hide from within. Tend the
root of our love and share its abundance.

Question not the faces and know I love you.

One seed, one life, one love
... and never did I wonder your return.

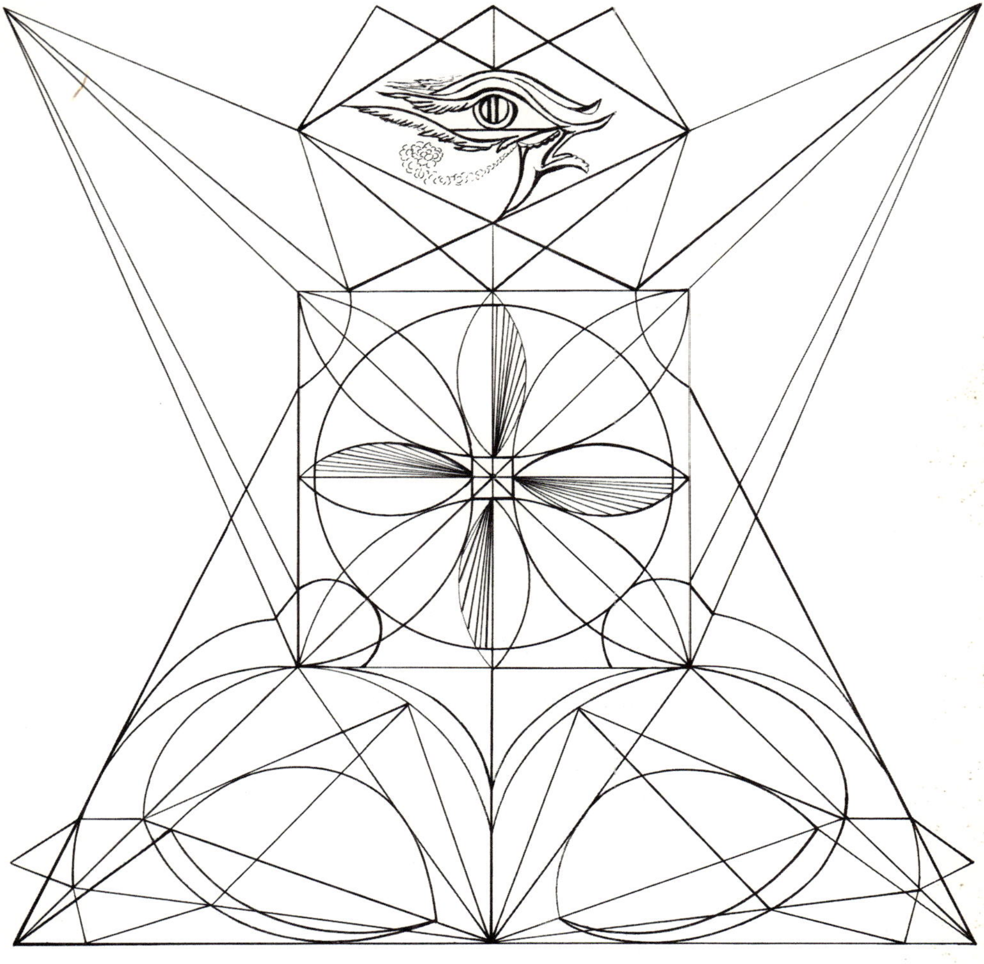

DETOUR AHEAD

BRIDGE CROSSING

FOR THOSE WHO SEE

If from the fruit of my tree you take ...
you may taste even the green I myself
tasted as sour ... while wanting for you
only the most pleasant of nectar

But life's tree ripens anew
            yields anew
            Therefore The Tree Bears

Envy not another's garden
but taste of your own nectar

If it be sour ... sweeten it
If it overflows ... let its kindness carry

Only from the Garden of Love
can the Seed of Understanding
be born anew

THE ENDLESS VOID

Had there not been
 an overabundance of rain
Had there not been
 a sunrise to look out upon
Had there not been
 the Chorten of the mountain

  We would have forever drifted
   the endless void

Had there not been
 the wing upon the wind
Had there not been
 the olive leafed in its branch
Had there not been
 His love beyond the darkness

  We would have forever drifted
   the endless void

Had the seed not accepted its rooting . . .

Had the rooting not accepted its stem . . .

Had the stem not accepted

Both thorn and leaf . . .

The Rose in

its entirety would never have ....BLOOMED

HOMEWARD

Two men crossing homeward
center stage
shadowing a bridge

Said the one
in a voice …
drowning,
"The load you carry falters not
your stride."

Said the one
in a voice …
lifting,
"I never carry more than the moment
in my stride."

... have traveled by foot
meditation
cerebellum dreams
unlocked doors by thought
golden beyond a key

There have been moments
when the dried date of the palm
has carried me
while hunger raced the mind
searching truth
through thundered storms
winging the eye of an eagle
crossing reality in cerebellum dreams

Still ... you are my story

When we comprehend
    the growth of another

We see the true distance
    we ourselves have traveled

Let us not walk

within the shadows of our lives

But stand afront

knowing we are the casters

Most people spend a lifetime
    preparing for the box

While others spend a lifetime
    preparing for the lift

The Self should never run away from its Self

As the Self is unto itself its carrier

Strength is not in
TENSION

Strength is in
FLEXIBILITY

up
The building of one's walkway leads ... or
down

Depending on its builder's point of view

WINTER'S CHILD

Seasons change ...
all too soon summer's gone
and once again I find myself
holding back Winter's Child

The warmth of summer removed
grounds the wings upon which I fly
while others cross the threshold
welcoming change
like the warmth of a beautiful woman

Soon the rains will come
washing clean the mountainside
leaving summer's laughter
and once again, I find myself
holding back Winter's Child

By summer's night shall ride the moon
awakening all my yesterdays

Winter's Child ...
Race the stallion from out his loneliness
Voice the wind upon the mystery you ride
Thunder your riverbeds
Crack wide the pathway through the mountain
and I shall ride free
I shall ride *FREE*
and welcome Winter's Child

It's been said my friend
by a far more prolific tongue than mine,
"A rose is a rose is a rose."

But it's true my friend
a rose is a rose for those
who can see the rose in their lives.

The very young are the buds of tomorrow.

Spring's newly bloomed petals forever
cascade a kaleidoscope rainbow,
a perfume no garden could bloom without.

The not so young, yet not so old
balance the stem of the rose.
Their love pollinates the everlasting bloom.

The majestic stately roses of yesteryear,
like autumn leaves, bloom forever
in the solitude of the mind.

The bloom is flowered anew
by the holder when he but sees
a rose is a rose is a rose ...
when he beholds the rose he holds
in his life.

SINCERITY

Awareness played itself laughing
from across the room
watching the oncoming faces
unaware of an awareness
as pretense moved the atmosphere
sponging here and there a giggle
holding a tight rein on the putdown

Hellos found themselves
echoed only by the oncoming
Clicking glasses added rhythm to the music
drowning out the small talk
held aloft by the ear of awareness

Time held the upper hand
smoothly concealed
faced by the young
dressing the mirror in vanity
while Merlin watched
looking out, waiting … waiting …
w-a-i-t-i-n-g for *SINCERITY*
to enter the room

Time the lost moments
Me, I wouldn't know where to begin

Most of us
In some way or another
Find conflict with everyday time

My father was the same ... but
He believed it to be more important
To say hello to someone —
Than the time it would take

ONE ... ONE AND THE SAME

ONE looks at *ZERO*
ZERO looks at *ONE*
ONE passes through *ZERO*
ZERO moves not

The mystery of life held open
While *ONE* makes the perfect cross

What's the difference between a caterpillar
And a butterfly?
No difference
They're *ONE . . . ONE* and the same

What's the difference between life and death?
No difference

They're *ONE . . . ONE* and the same

How does a man differ from a caterpillar?
ONE cocoons
ONE transcends
Both evolve from *ONE* passing through *ZERO*
Evolving *ONE* out of *ONE* into *ONE*

ONE fulfilling the mystery of life
ONE ... ONE and the same

UPON ITS GROWTH

DESIRE WOULD WITHER

IF ALL COULD BE TOLD

He who seeks the GOLDEN RING

must reach for it

man

Crooked

A

Tall

Feet

Ten

Standing

There may appear

Virtuous

The

Woman

Called

A

Whore

To follow a river winding........................ *LEADS*

Crooked

May

Appear

Its

Beginning

Middle

Its

End

But

Never

Its

Empty ....ing

For only God can truly judge a man

To lay an egg
        not easy

Harder still
        to crack it from within

To face the *Light Glorious*
        yet horrifying to seed one's Seed

To answer one's self in question
        bilging wide closed doors

Daring to face the Master
        freeing emotion

To face the *Light Glorious*
        yet horrifying the learning
        in facing one's Seed
        seeding one's life

SOMEWHERE THERE'S A RIVER

Somewhere there's a river
That wants to be free
River, river, river
Keep callin' me

Someday we'll find that river, Brother
Just you wait and see
Someday we'll find that river, Sister
Just you wait and see

Gabriel, oh Gabriel

The river you seek is near
Never far beyond your reach
The river you seek will lead you
To the great stream

Seeking through the hardest of stone
Truth frees itself
And the river flows
The river flows to the great stream

Somewhere there's a river
That wants to be free
River, river, river
Keep callin', keep callin' me

Someday we'll find that river, Brother
Just you wait and see
Someday we'll find that river, Sister
Together, we'll set the river free

The husking down
of the corner barricade
is all good and fine
when replaced by *STABILITY*
... balancing ...
TRADITION

L I E S fall like raindrops
stormed by a solicit tongue
lobbying its platform
... candy-appled
eaten by the
U N I N F O R M E D

Echoes of a lost yesterday
Right or wrong
Need to be placed in balance

Lost souls face a sunrise
Darkened by hunger
While bleakness sponges every raindrop
Blooming the cactus flower

Self pride hides
In the arms of an empty belly
Shadowing the dust
Searching out water holes

The forgotten road

THE MARKETPLACE

Greed on sale at any price
A bargain to behold
        Step right up
        Don't be shy
        Fleece 'em down
        Turn 'em out
        Wink 'em in the eye

Greed on sale at any price
        The marketplace
        The marketplace
        Countered
        Tagged
        Falsified

Leftover promises newly wrapped
        Vigilant its keeper

Vintagers of yesterday
        Vis à vis
                Once a lost walker

THOSE WHO HAVE MUSIC

Those who have music
Stand afront
Those who have a song to sing ... sing
Those who feel together we can find a better way
Stand afront
Stand up
Stand up and sing

Don't look back in bitterness
Don't look back in revenge
Free us
Lead us
Show us how together we can find a better way

Tell it like you feel it
Feel it like you tell it
Pass the good word
Pass the good word around

Those who have music
Stand afront
Those who have a song to sing ... sing
Those who feel together we can find a better way
Stand afront
Stand up
Stand up and sing

a hurricane
hit our beach
all the umbrellas
upped and blew away

umbrellas
chairs
tin-canned echoes
leftover promises
you name it
fat cats and all
even those hiding
upped theirs
and blew away

a hurricane
hit our beach
sometime ...
yesterday
all the umbrellas
upped and blew away

keep believing, Miss Watkins ...
never seen more leftover yesterdays
sad faces and all ... up and blow away

Hanging
F
A
C
E
S
can be fun

Grumpy voices too
B
U
T

Crabby people
never see
T
H
E
M
S
E
L
V
E
S
the way other

people do

We've all dressed up too many times
not to notice
we're wearing a yesterday mask

Surely here or there a wrinkle
wouldn't really matter
but Lord only knows
a healthy laugh might just c-r-a-c-k
the whole damn veneer

Yesterday you were like an all-day sucker
passed from hand-to-hand to lick

But today you're like an ice cream cone
too bad you got soggy . . .
. . . .

Who are we who see
                    see nothing

Who are we who damn
                    damn visigothic

Who are we who cage
                    cage revivification

Once I gave my words
Not knowingly ... fool thought
To the bitter bite of envy
My young truly given of warmth
Oh, so newly born, faced now
    The bitter dormant ear of envy

Had I dressed my words too nakedly
To penetrate the cold, deaf ear
Had the furrowing of my cultivation
Been fervent
And to what degree of cold
    Could the newborn now endure

Word-by-word I planted them
Through the icy polar cap
Seeking to tap
The warmth of stability
Held lost in bondage
    The vestige held its facade

The word sung
Sings a lingered sound
    Unto the voicer

Let not his tree
Be frostbitten
If he not be strong enough
To withstand the taste of its fruit
Sweet or sour ... steadfast the rudder
    Or he but bears a dormant tree

The seed of truth
Will withstand
The iciest of glaciers
Burn fast the driest of sands
    In its Awakening

A foot laid heavy above it
Thought crushed
    Permanates it

THE ICE AGE IS MELTING

The young here and in Alaska
the young throughout the world
should not be held in bondage.
They are the very bridge over which
we shall hand in hand cross tomorrow.

Their minds are the new turbulent Awakening.
Our new river of life is on the move. The Ice
Age is melting. No damming will stop its flow.

To advocate drugs I do not, but the Ice Age is
melting. The rust of a million lifetimes past
has creviced a *light:*

Automation
A universe beckons
Tomorrow's dreams ...
Seen world-wide on the moment
... Awakens the Seed of Understanding

Our fathers' fathers' plow, decayed of yesteryears
— seeded through love — cannot withstand the mighty
thrust charged against it in an evolution of an
electronic age.

Beware of fire if there not be water.

The Ice Age awakens the universal mind.
To our children go our dreams. Man has evolved full
circle from year one into zero. Energy into rhythm;
darkness into light; the moon is in perfect balance.
Negative into positive; yin into yang; love seeding
the heart ... or he but faces his own eclipse.
The Awakening is now. The Seed of Understanding has
been furrowed anew. Are we not the very Seed crying
out for water?

As yesterday was but a dream, tomorrow was never born.
We together are the living moment, passing through
our Awakening.

The vacuumed generation
    isolation
    emptiness
    a space devoid of matter
    creating pressure

The vacuumed generation
    imposed negative
    a light
    a single step

Ancestral descent
    from within the line
    fragmenting isolation

THE LIFTING OF THE MASK

I have listened with heart
to stories told by men daring
to open tomorrow's door
I have listened
and in the listening I have seen

Fear holds us
like a child
clings to a teddy bear
while we of the day
harvest bitterness
and upon this nipple
we feed our young

How far past the moment
dare one travel
eluding the self
raping the harvest
knowing the moment of truth
awaits his arrival
in the lifting of the mask

LOOK AFTER TOMORROW FOR ME

Was it all a nightmare
played out in a jungle
defending blindness?

I've spilled the rice from out my bowl
    too many times
    not to have noticed the sparrows.

High upon the hill voices are calling ...
    a sweeter lullaby
    never trumpeted the nightingale.

        Look after tomorrow for me
        knowing I'm every son
        in every field.
        No footprint upon tomorrow's walk
        shall I leave
        beyond your remembrance.
        No longer will tears roll
        beyond my eyes.
        How can I touch blame?
        Only the living can answer.

Loneliness ends defending ...
    coldness surmounts the wooded walls
    distance fades in emptiness ... crying out ...

Make friends with tomorrow for me
    knowing I'm every son in every field.

I've spilled the rice from out my bowl
    too many times ... not to have noticed ...

the sparrows.

Stillness cradled in silence
Silences the moment
Sweetens the sounds heard
Heard by the early morning ear

The giant surf thunders a lingered yawn
Rolls back the mist
While trumpeters high above the cliffs
Feather their songs

Stillness cradled in silence
Hears *HIS* voice
Silences the moment
Brightens the Awakening
A new day, a new dawn

Yonder tolls a bell
Moans a black angus
Jumps the startled newborn fawn
Heard in silence
Seen by the early morning ear

When a man listens with his thoughts
    he hears
When he sees beyond the self mirrored
    he visions anew
When he houses the self beyond self
    he need not walk in darkness

How green the thought of spring
    before summer

The Song of Life is yours for the singing
You are the song from which you sing
You are the love of what you bring
You are the moment in which He walks
Therefore, let not your image be distorted

Times are a-changin'
What's in today's out tomorrow
What's out tomorrow's back in today
That's why I'm holdin' on
Lookin' out, wingin' free

I'm not orange, red, or yellow
Copper-white, pink-brown-black
Or even cherry-green
But you can see me
In all the colors of the rainbow
If you like

I'm not orange, red, or yellow
Sky-blue-grey
Or even frog toad mud on a rainy day
I'm just me
Holdin' on, lookin' out, wingin' free
But you can see me
In all the colors of the rainbow
All the colors of the rainbow
If you like

LOVE is the very light
cradling the candle
searching out the darkness
listening to silence
calling aloud your name

You are called by name
as viewed by others
You are all of life to me
colored by thought
I ask not from where you come
only happy for your arrival

When time has parched its shadow
beyond the breath
... as in the now
I'll hold out my love
rendering it silently
never leaving you
... beyond your remembrance

LOVE

Love is an agony of pain
It feels better than ice cream tastes
It's the shadow of a hand saying goodbye
The tear that chokes a laugh
Or the naked dream that waits

It's the friend who knows the inner you
The voice of belief
Love's an ever-opening of doors ...

It's the eye that listens
To the sound of your hello
Or the beginning of losing one's self
Finding one's self through love
Never ending

Knew a man once
Who held onto love
Believing it would fly away ...

He was right

Who knows
Where a woman hides her tears
Or how many she can store
But break her heart ...
How endless
How endless
The pour

HOUSE OF SOMBER DREAMS

Barks aloud the dog
Magnificent the persian
Stalking emptiness
Where once laughter rang

In the house of somber dreams
Two lonely rivers run
Two lonely rivers running to nowhere

Time the moments lost in silence
Promises forgotten
Driving happiness away

Lidded windows
Jostled rocking
Elbowed chairs
Darting eyes
Searching a landing

Warmly blowing muted horns
Sounding *"Auld Lang Syne"*
Rattles not the pilfered drum

In the house of somber dreams
Where boredom sleeps
Never hearing the calling of the day
Two lonely rivers running to nowhere
Through the misunderstanding of the day

The awareness speaks
To the man who listens
While holding today
In the palm of his hand

If you are given a hundred years
Some only a day
Live the moment
Love the moment
Before those beautiful moments
Slip away

Time slips through our shadows
As easily
As she removes our days

WHY RACE TIME

HE'S AN ENDLESS TROTTER

A visionary is one who tracks the footprint
of a forward runner —
which would appear to have imaged itself
in a yesterday

Truth by its very name surfaces not
Till we care *why*
There are two sides to every story

I'll leave my *MASK*
at the door
You'll recognize it
Don't be late ...
please ... Don't be late

RETURN THE NECTAR

Just leave me alone
Let me be
Let me be what I need to be
Not what you think I should be
In the name of God, let me be

Lonely unto myself I may be
But finding myself will set me free

As a child traveler passes through time
I alone face my Awakening

It's time for me to turn around
Knowing what's up is really down

Patternless waves swirl around
Autumn colored leaves trumpet color to sound

The universe beckons like a distant star
Sounds move in to beam me afar

Just leave me alone — pass meaninglessly

Crystals of color, minerals of time
Move through me — remove me — pure energy
No longer am I
Ego of a past but faded away

Beamed by the cradle hum of the soul
Eager to nourish pure love once again
From the bosom of the eternal
God-given soul

Flowered melodies ...
Sung ... will sing anew
The lyrics of my life
Return ... return I will
The raft but passes
Not alone ... am *i*

Long after autumn has faded
I'll remember the warmth
Of early spring
I'll remember ... I'll remember

Long after my bloom has flourished
I'll taste again the nectar
The sweet nectar of youth
And once again ... I'll remember

I'll remember
The Majestic Stately Yellow Roses
Beautiful yellow roses
But most of all
In the warmth of early spring
I'll remember ... I'll remember you

A door easily opened
Finds itself seldom used

A door cracked in light
Brings a man forward

A locked door
UNHINGES THE MIND

The sign read:

Happiness Inside
  Welcome
    Please Come In
      Open Wide The Door

An enchanted cottage in need of a lover

Browse awhile, dust away
Behold all you've ever dreamed ...
All that glitters a sunken treasure
Carry away ... or leave

Venture through stories
Never read before
Stay awhile ... a lifetime ... stay longer ...
Welcome ... open wide the door

A cottage enchanted
A White Flower to behold
Nestled in a garden
Where only love can see

Turn as many pages
Leafed Golden upon the moment
Random the embrace
Till desire holds you in its warmth
... As would the babe upon the breast
A sanctuary ... silent in the listening

Flowering before your eyes a dwelling
The likes never seen before

Your story *AWAKENS ...*
And there behold thy truthful page
In thy knowing of thyself

Stay awhile ... a lifetime ... stay longer..................................

I've seen a thousand
And one sunsets
I've walked within cities
Floating in the sky
But never have I seen
More love
Or felt more alive
Than this moment
Being here with you

I've talked with voices
From far, far beyond belief
I've even danced in silence
And questioned it not
But never have I seen
More love
Or felt more alive
Than this moment
Being here with you

For each day I had lost
I find no one was to blame
For each story without ending
I needed you to tell it to
Like sand sifting through
An hour glass
Time holds for me
A new beginning
Now that I've found you

S
Dec
25

Give till the calendar days of your mind
turn to zero
Walk from beneath a waterfall
and buoyant your head in the crossing

Give till a voice sings aloud your name
Close not a door behind you
but see the reflection of your other face
in the forward look
He who may look the devil
may one day face you with an angel's smile

Hold fast to your love
it will always live young in the giving
Listen to a tear sounding your name
it may one day ring a bell
the one you rang in the giving

Let your candle altar a glow
to light the way for the voices
that one day will sing your name

Voices may ring aloud ... I've gone away
Hear little of what slumbers in disbelief
When you feel lost, or thorned by the rose
you pick ... believe ... and in your belief
i shall come to you

Let my silent voicing brighten your way
like a candle running the dark corners
blowing emptiness away

I'll stay
I'll wait
I'll live for you
As long as you need me I'll stay
I'll stay beyond the edge of darkness

Our Dance ...
the very flame
consumes the foliage
in its nakedness
unashamed
bedding beyond walls
seeding the mind

By the very breath given thought
Our love shall race the wind aging time
Corinthian ... Ionic ... Doric ...
known pillars of time
Future Spectrum
carry me where only you can
... and in your heart
I need never go away

A touching devoid of instrument
rhythmed partnership
in the baring of pages

Our oneness ...
in the sensitivity
unveiling the mask

THE LOVERS

only time has wrinkled
not you my love ... not *i*

I shall from time to time
awaken you beyond the written word.
When the dotted i finds the self
shelved in darkness, I shall ever
so gently whisper my need of you.

The acceptance of one's self
Collaging one's daily dream
The cardinal acceptance

Tempering, moulding, furnacing
Thought balanced in emotion
Icing the fire chambers in the giving
The cardinal acceptance of one's self

Fulfillment through outward giving
Not to be weighed

The clay furnacing the outer mould
Purifying the inner soul

Through the inner chambers
One can reach true happiness
Lost in his awareness
While passing through the ego id
Of selfishness

Becoming one with one in the giving
As easy as a smile or saying hello
One truly lives in the giving

He then receives
The daily cardinal acceptance
His life

It Feels Good To Be Needed

It Feels Better To Know It

The last chapter — The End
The last chapter — The Beginning
The Beginning of the End written
Yet not read

The story of forever
The last chapter
Never shall it be read

A lifetime of pages
Turned one by one
A billion dreams
Of that tomorrow

Stabilizing the rudder
Canvasing, reinforcing the header
Weathering a thousand calls to battle
Praying a lifetime — the last chapter
Never shall it be read

A hundred million laughs floating by
Some on tears
The remembrance of one's aloneness
Yet the very thought itself alive

Birth a dream unto the dreamer
If he not be the dream
He therefore not be the dreamer

The Beginning never Beginning
The Beginning never Ending
I AM has been written
Therefore, *I AM* ...

Beyond tomorrow
Where no man walks
Beyond his shadow
From which he leaves ....

What would you have me say?
Would you have me tell you lies
I myself do not believe?

In truth, I am the man in the arena
A man learning ... from you
In need of you.

Would you have me tell you lies
I myself do not believe?